Paws Healing The Earth

RIVER PAW PRESS

Paws Healing The Earth
Copyright © River Paw Press

First Edition: 2021

ISBN: 978-1-7366871-0-9

Concept, Anthology Selection and the Editor's Note
Copyright © Kalpana Singh-Chitnis, 2021

Individual Poems and Translations
Copyrights © Individual Poets and Translators

Layout, Book Cover © Silent River
Cover Photo: © Mona El Falaky (Public Domain)
Copy Editing: Kalpna Singh-Chitnis and Nirvan Chitnis

All rights reserved. No part of this publication may be reproduced, distributed, or transmitted in any form or by any means, including photocopying, recording, or other electronic or mechanical methods, without the prior written permission of the publisher, except in the case of brief quotations embodied in critical reviews and certain other noncommercial uses permitted by copyright law.

RIVER PAW PRESS
USA
www.riverpawpress.com

Paws Healing The Earth

Edited by

Kalpna Singh-Chitnis

River Paw Press

Acknowledgment

Thanks to all contributing poets of *Paws Healing The Earth* for their
sublime poetry and Mona El Falaky for her outstanding photograph, which
makes the cover of this anthology. A very special thanks to editor-intern
Nirvan Chitnis for his endless hours of work during the Pandemic in
putting this book together. Amata Natasha Goldie and Shashwat Chitnis,
thank you for your valuable suggestions and believing in this book.
Above all, a bow to the sacredness of our extended animal-family
at home and in the wilderness for inspiring this exceptional anthology.

For Troy

(April 20th 2006 - November 7th 2018)

Paws Healing The Earth

CONTENTS

Editor's Note   11

Jonel Abellanosa   17
Bloodhound
Cheetah

Shanta Acharya   19
Living Without Cleopatra
Happines

Leticia Austria   21
Moment Out of Time
Rondo

Mark Blickley   23
Mysterious Waters of the Naked and Nervous

Betty Burton   25
Spitfire

Jenna Butler   26
The Cougar

Xánath Caraza   27
Huitzil
Damp Smile

Jennifer Carr   29
A Prayer for the Owl Spirit

Joshua Corwin   30
Thank You for the Rainbow
When I Think of You in Tears

Douglas K Currier   34
Notification
Soledad

Candice Louisa Daquin   36
For Halo

April Garcia   42
For Stella

Claudia Gary   44
Sapphics For a Crow

Amata Natasha Goldie   46
You Once Were Many
The Feline Teacher

Albert Gonzales   50
Floppy-Eared Free Loader

Marian Haddad   52
Satchel
Bonnie

Lois P. Jones   55
Smokey in the Year of Our Feline, 2099
The Goodmorninggoat Says

Zilka Joseph   57
All Our Little Ones?
Black Swan
In Taos Pueblo, Suddenly

Abhay K.   63
Ten Haiku from Madagascar

Diane Kendig   65
Midsummer Night Walk
The Geese at the Prison

John C. Mannone   67
Her Name Was Candy
Raccoons Can't Fly

Ellyn Maybe   70
Kiko in Greenville

Christopher Merrill   71
Two Samoyeds

Jagari Mukharjee   73
The Takins At Thimpu

Kunwar Narain   74
In Krakow Zoo

William O'Daly   75
Bears in Autumn
Heron Dances Over the World

Yogesh Patel   77
Did you ask the tree?

Saleem Peeradina   78
Blueprint
Donkey

Robert Pinsky   80
Door

Connie Post   81
Advice to the Dog Sitter
The Night Before Surgery
"Terriers Hold Grudges" Our veterinarian says

Jennifer Reeser   87
I Have No Horse
The Mockingbird
"No, not the monkey, Mother, but the stag..."

Susan Rogers   90
Billy
Blessing at Fair Oaks

MistyRose™   92
Rough Win
Turf Wag-ing

Minal Sarosh   94
A Peacock's Feather
Honey

Kedarnath Singh   96
Animal Fare
Five Puppies

Kalpna Singh-Chitnis   98
Paws Healing The Earth
Epiphany
Naming
Red Fox Family

Adrian Slonaker   104
Encounter in Whitehorse
The Wolf On My Right Arm

Donna Snyder 106
Doggerel for Lily
Lover boy

Megha Sood 110
Blue Eye of the Magpie

Janaka Stagnaro 111
Animals Within Us
The Cow
Frey the Cat on a Solstice Night

Melissa Studdard 114
Tour of Grief
Because Deathbolts Illuminate the Wonderstorm
There's a brightness folded into every bird

Ambika Talwar 118
Gaze of Horse – Lure of Wholiness

Leslie Thomas 120
Where you used to

Lee Upton
The Persistence of Torture 122

Contributors' Bio Notes 129

Editor's Note

How profoundly animals inspire our creativity, *Paws Healing The Earth* anthology is just one example of it.

Seventy-six animal poems by forty-four poets woven into one thread allow us to discover our collective consciousness in pure brilliance essential to our survival and well-being.

You may ask, "What inspired the *Paws Healing The Earth?*"

It all began with Troy, our family dog, a Lhasa Apso. This breed of mountain dog was named after Tibet's capital, Lhasa. We adopted Troy from the Orange County Animal Shelter in Orange, California, where he had come as a stray. He was two when we rescued him. We always wondered about Troy's origin, his first name, who his parents and owners were, and if he remembered any of them.

Troy's loss was apparent in his sad eyes when we first met him at the animal shelter. I tried to imagine his pain and made sure he was compensated for all his losses in his new home. He grew up with my children, and we treated him as the youngest child in our family.

It is said that *Lhasa Apsos are fallen Buddhist monks who incarnate to live in places where Dharma flourishes so they can continue on their spiritual journey.*

Our home was a sanctuary for Troy, and he was a master meditator. He would sit silently for hours at his favorite spots. He loved being in the backyard, liking the coolness of grass under his belly and gentle winds ruffling his hair. He had a white coat, a perfect gait, and a majestic appearance.

While walking, Troy would make frequent stops to sense the energy around him. Sometimes he would sit down in the middle of the way, refusing to walk until he had finished doing his Shaman things. I guess it was Troy's way of practicing walking meditation, stopping to focus on his breathing in between his laps, and moving at his own pace.

Our family, friends, and neighbors would often compliment that they have never heard Troy barking or running around. They were charmed by his calm presence and the soothing effect he had on everyone who touched him. Their testimonies earned Troy's nickname, the Monk Doggie. When we did Yoga, Troy would lay down on the rug to do his *Doga*! He loved vegetarian food. However, he ate everything recommended for a dog to stay healthy.

Troy had an extraordinary sense of reading others' energy and the ability to channel his own energy to others. On days I felt overwhelmed, he spoke to me in his language to make sure I was okay. He would put his face on my feet to calm me down. The days I was sad, he would look at me with concerns in his eyes. He would sit in my lap and cuddle with me under the blanket.

For an independent dog like him, it was a rare display of love and care.

Troy showed his approval and disapproval by being grave or making the "Umh" sound when he felt stressed. He also knew when he made mistakes. He would pull a guilty face when caught red-handed. He didn't damage things in our house or soiled the carpet but liked to play with toilet paper, for which he was scolded many times. We made several videos of Troy's mischiefs and took a million photos of him, now his memories.

Sometimes I think I didn't rescue Troy; Troy recused me. He was a light in the darkest phase of my life.

When I rescued him, I turned vegetarian. I began to see my connection with the rest of the planet at a much deeper level. Troy inspired me to create a particular program at the Silent River Film Festival called "Cinema For Causes," which earned the support of many animal rights and environmental activists and celebrities like Sharon Stone, Jorja Fox, Julliet West, and others. This program raises awareness by showcasing cinema related to various causes and providing active support, including charitable donations.

Troy guided me back upon the path I was meant to travel.

When this canine teacher arrived, he taught me the most profound lesson — Love and Compassion for all living beings.

His departure taught me another important lesson: Accepting the nature of Impermanence in everything that exists.

After a three-year battle with Cushing's disease, which stripped Troy of his vision at its onset, he passed away peacefully in his sleep at a time when I was traveling twelve thousand miles away from home. I wasn't able to say my final goodbye to him. I still regret my decision to travel to China and India at a time when Troy was fragile. He knew I was gone, and it was time for him to leave. Had I not been traveling, perhaps my care, and will, would have kept him alive for a few more days or months, who knows.

I don't know for sure when my love for animals began. I guess it was always there. Growing up in India, I saw animals around me all the time. Not only the pet dogs, parrots, cows, and chickens we had at home but goats, monkeys, buffaloes, you name it, coexisting with us, walking down the streets, in temples and orchards.

In my hometown, one can get rare sightings of cows and buffaloes posturing near the bonfire on the roadside, where the laborers and rickshaw pullers hang around to find jobs, and the homeless survive the winter.

In India, animals are expected everywhere. Bullock carts and horse wagons share space on the road with regular traffic. Pigeons and peacocks surprisingly pay a visit to our homes. I grew up seeing bears, monkeys, and cobra shows on the roadside. At the time, it seemed fun, but now looking back, I think it was sad to use animals for shows and circus. I also rode camels in the deserts of Rajasthan and elephants in my home state, Bihar, on the bank of the Phalgu river during the Chhat Puja; a Vedic festival dedicated to the sun, the protector of the environment.

In India, there are temples for animals everywhere. Not only the cows, but dogs, monkeys, snakes, and several other animals are worshiped. Almost all Sanātan deities, who personify some aspect of nature and human existence, have an animal-vehicle.

Shiva travels on a bull and coils a snake around his neck, Vishnu sleeps on a bed of Cobra, guarding him in his sleep, and Brahma journeys on a swan. Krishna is seen with his cow and Hanuman, the divine monkey, on Rama's side.

The earliest reference of human and animal interactions is found in the *Rig Veda*, the oldest Indian text. In the hymn (10.86), the Rain God Indra tells his unhappy wife, Indrani (who didn't like the idea of sharing the offerings brought for her husband by people with a monkey!) that we must strive to coexist with animals peacefully. Later, he invited the monkey to his palace to share his offerings with him.

When Fixian traveled to India, he mentioned in his travel accounts — "Throughout the whole country, the people do not kill any living creature, nor drink intoxicating liquor, nor eat onions or garlic... In that country, they do not keep pigs and fowls, and do not sell live cattle; in the markets there are no butchers' shops and no dealers in intoxicating drink." (*The Travels of Fa-Hsien, A Record of the Buddhistic Kingdoms*, translated by James Legge (Oxford: Clarendon Press, 1886).

India is no longer the same. Over the centuries, it has embraced the influences of foreign cultures that arrived in India with invasions and subjugation of the country, changing people's eating habits to a large extent. However, there are still more vegetarian people in India than in any other country in the world.

My love for animals turned into compassion, has much to do with my upbringing. My grandfather from my mother's side managed the Princely State of Tekari. The King of Tekari, Maharaja Gopal Sharan Singh, loved hunting, and my grandfather would often accompany the Maharaja on his hunting trips.

After independence from the British rule, the white men, kings, and queens were gone, but the love for hunting stayed in my family. Guns, rifles, and trophies hung from the walls of our homes. My father took upon hunting as a sport, and as a child, I went on several hunting trips with him. This is when I fell in love with the beauty of the forest that still sings in me.

However, sometimes I feel sad to recollect my forest adventures with my father and his friends. The blood of animals still traumatizes me. The hunting party would fire shots in the sky, and innocent birds would rain down with bullet holes in their bodies. Some who were still alive, I would nurse their wounds and save them. I would close my eyes and plug fingers into my ears when the animals ran for their lives, as shots were fired at them. A female deer, hunted by my father, had milk dripping from her breast. Her fawns escaped, but their images still haunt me. My father never ate the animals he killed. It was an act of repentance; not enough?

Hunting was banned in India under the Wildlife Protection Act in 1972. However, it took longer to strictly implement the law. But the forests and animals I loved were finally protected, and a part of the earth went on its journey to healing.

Paws Healing The Earth poetry anthology is a modest effort to raise awareness about the environment and animal rights. The contributing poets, through their poems, discover the sacredness of our natural environment and honor all the animals who share the planet with us. The poems in this anthology thoughtfully penned by the poets are meditations on animals' lives, giving rise to compassion in our hearts, much needed to bring the changes we want to see to protect animals, domestic or wild, and their abode. This anthology is a celebration of all animals and wildlife, healing the earth with their presence.

Kalpna Singh-Chitnis

"Until one has loved an animal, a part of one's soul remains unawakened."

–Anatole France

Paws Healing The Earth

Bloodhound

By Jonel Abellanosa

I may look avuncular, flap-dangle ears
clue of my submissive love. I don't look
eager, but docility makes me a dissembler.
One sniff, and we're clear. Teach me,
be my trainer. I know who is evil.
I'm gentle, I'm analyzing. I tilt my head
to ask. Give it time, you'll see.
No one hides from me.

No one gets away with a crime.
I'll show you where the body is buried.
I'll lead you to the unidentified subject's
hiding place. You catch and take credit.
I wag my tail. You reunite children
to parents. They'll embrace with happy
tears, thanking you with love. I appreciate
a treat every once in a while.
Quiet moments of chewing
make me grateful, my heart
bigger than your kindness.

Cheetah

By Jonel Abellanosa

Distance like the optic nerve, swept
in a split second. I've been running wild
since you're still a twinkle in God's eye,
legs aerodynamic as neurons. In my practice
seconds swarm like synapses, wind conspiring
with pleasure, angling easily as geometry.
Desire's equations like antelopes. Retinas
filter what I let you see. I sprint like thoughts,
four feet off the ground most of the time,
paths bridging like cochlear nerves.
I like to race with them who can be faster,
whose intuitions are receptors. They smell
false notes like hounds, after precision
as prey, chasing the next question.

Living Without Cleopatra

for Jaysinh Birjépatil

By Shanta Acharya

From her couch Cleopatra saw the bronze full moon
hanging like Captain Ahab's doubloon,
high on the mast of heaven,
reward for sighting the forsworn Other, the enemy within.

The moon was almost exactly at dead noon
in the sky-clock of the window when she woke in pain.
At the end of her memory there was dampness,
years of darkness as she struggled to remember.

The scene in the distance was an advent calendar –
windows lighted with goodwill messages.
The clock inside Cleopatra was ticking too fast
as she dreamed and sighed for her Antony.

He had been a sprightly puppy before disease and age
lathered him with fat. He breathed his last with his shiny
nose seeking her paws, their communication encompassing
the vastness of time and space. As age withered her
poor demented Cleopatra went barking mad,
baying at the moon as if she saw her Antony there.

One moonstruck night she sighted the forsworn enemy
and lunged at the double moon swimming in the pool.
Breathless, out of habit, she drowned, howling for Antony,
her whole world buried in the moving, waning moon.

Happiness

By Shanta Acharya

The rivalry was palpable as they hurled
abuse, called each other Fat Cat, Starving Dog –
our children no longer little, drawing
boundaries, exploring their limits, strengths
and kindnesses, pretending to be all grown up –
until saved by strays who adopted us.
The naming ceremony was the hardest of all.
After the quarantine and requisite procedures,
it took days for our daughter to decide if her dog
who followed her home should be named
Yudhisthira, Ringo, Rufus, Fala or Mister.
Yu it was for he would not respond to any other.
And our son who really wanted a polydactyl feline
kept addressing his cat by different names –
Snowball, Tyke, Marcus, Major, settling for Babou
when the call provoked a smile and an arching purr.
Happiness is watching them all play together –
Babou's philosophical chuckle on seeing a bird,
Yu enjoying the thrill of a chase, pursuing
artful squirrels – leaving us laughing, clapping,
cheering, holding us enthralled in their fold.

Moment Out of Time

By Leticia Austria

The day was still,
as if carved of crystal.
An almost
imperceptible breeze,
a single dead leaf
wafting
towards grass. . .
it seemed nothing
would ever move again.
The sweet stray
tuxedo cat crouched
beside a bush
stone-still,
eyeing a dove.

Sudden blur of wing, sure flight to a high rose arch;
cat's eyes following, bright flash of emerald---

stillness was broken
and the day took a breath.

Rondo
By Leticia Austria

In spring
the dog across the alley
gathers all the patio furniture and piles it
in the middle of the yard. Sometimes
he wears a chair as a hat and runs
round.

In summer
the grandchildren come. They play
with the dog and chase him. He barks
when they laugh and when they scatter
the patio furniture
round the yard.

In autumn
the rains make pools in the patio chairs
and the dog rolls
in the leaves that scatter
round the yard.

In winter
the dog across the alley
serenades me in the night
with his doleful
rounds.

Mysterious Waters of the Naked and Nervous

By Mark Blickley

She began her life along with nine-thousand seven hundred and fourteen other siblings in the shallowest part of the water, just four days after she was laid as a jelly egg attached to a fern leaf that bent over the water. On the seventh day she sallied to neighboring weeds using a very circular route. She quietly clung to these weeds and watched with terror as her brothers and sisters were repeatedly attacked by sharp beaked birds that swooped down and chewed the helpless tadpoles, devouring the membrane that covered their gills and necks.

She was one of the few tadpoles to survive to day ten when she officially became a tiny pitch-black pollywog with a tail that continuously wiggled and a small round mouth that she opened for the first time as her horny jaws scraped across tiny plants, searching for something to eat. She greedily swallowed the microscopically small animals she found inside the ooze of the pond bottom and the slime that clung to the pond's surface.

While devouring a particularly tasty pond ooze meal, she was horrified to witness some of her tadpole brothers and sisters actually eating each other. It disturbed her to think that her siblings were extending their bellies by swallowing their extended family.

She was mostly tail with a fine stippling of gold. Within the next twenty-four hours she was breathing through the two gills at each side of her throat. Hind legs suddenly sprouted, rounded buds that soon turned into toes. She began to use her legs as well as her tail for swimming and was amazed at how fast she could propel herself in the water, away from murderous dive-bombing birds of color.

Her courage was first demonstrated when she successfully attacked a black fish that had menaced her for more than three hours. She sucked on the fish fins until they were ragged although it wasn't anger or self-defense that motivated the fish attack as much as it was the tasty algae trapped within its fins.

But it did feel good to be able to destroy instead of being destroyed.

Spitfire

By Betty Burton

Imagine our surprise
Finding you there at the bottom of our porch steps
Such a sweet little thing
Until you hissed at us like you were a guard cat
My first words were
"Spitfire we ain't taken that crap"
Her mother had given birth under a building
Along with two others.
Her mom brought one
And Spitty was left behind, never experiencing love
My son was first to hold and cuddle her
It was a scorching July day
Suddenly there came a roaring
"Wind" my son yelled as we headed inside
The wind gained strength blowing everything around
Thunder roared and lightning flashed
Spitfire stayed on the porch
Running outside Dustin scooped Spitfire up
She had barely been holding on
Together we three weathered Derecho
The storm helped Spitfire to trust and love us unconditional
She was the first cat that I loved back
This feisty bundle of fur finally found her family.

The Cougar

By Jenna Butler

That winter, we found its careful tracks
set down in noiseless, deliberate span
beyond the fall of light from the cabin door,
the nimbus of all we'd circumscribed as ours.

Something keen about those spreading prints,
an excised gravitas in November snow,
not pressing bounds, but simply skeined
out past the visible, where all things lower

and vanish when the dusk comes frosting in.
It's a basic truth: we're nature-bound
to step from the path when the path is fair
for no other reason than the fact we doubt

what we've always known: that something's there
past the paralyzing edges of the safe and right.
There's something wilder unhinged in darkness:
the cougar, like the limber spine of night.

And the summer turns, and it dogs us still,
though the muskeg dries and refuses tracks.
There's a certain circling in these northern woods,
and the silence of the frogs is, itself, address.

When the cougar comes, that breathless weight
is the nighttime tearing, unwieldy, thin.
Not the din of frogs or the slough birds' chuckle,
but the exhale of winter on our June-damp skin.

Huitzil

By Xánath Caraza
Translated from the original Spanish by Sandra Kingery

Designs of clouds
share your dreams.

Ring out, melody of air,
at the crown of the ceiba tree.

I sense hummingbird's desire
in jungle mist.

Huitzil, huitzil, huitzil, huitzil!

Whispers, in full moon,
wind from the south.

Huitzil inhales memories
deep into his lungs

and warbles to the rhythm of leaves
that spill into the river.

Water from the mountain,
whirlpools and stones

carry the scent of the
hummingbird on its current.
No hummingbird can tame
the desires of the jungle.

Preserved in the heart,
in liquid gold, is my name.

Damp Smile

By Xánath Caraza
Translated from the original Spanish by Sandra Kingery

Cool sensation on skin,
damp smile.

The flight of the hummingbird is born
for the first time.

Early morning fluttering
emerges from the rock.

Blue-green hope
in natural springs.

Crystalline fountain reflects
early morning light.

Subtle dream imbibing
alongside immaculate angel's trumpet.

He cuts the wavy currents
of dense water with his beak.

A Prayer for the Owl Spirit

By Jennifer Carr

Might I be born a mighty bird
I would soar over mountains
look to the moon for direction and purpose
for an unseen spirit lives there
with unknown powers
eyes that can see through the darkest hours
the moon glow shining from above the tree line
outshining any shadows lurking
among the wonder of stars
even as the fullness of the moon fades
'O spirit continue to grace my wings with freedom
whether I travel near or far
let your presence be known
so that I may never be alone

Thank You for the Rainbow

—for Bogie
By Joshua Corwin

I love you,
but you shat on my shoe
with the rainbow.

I love you,
and you clearly love me
because you told me
where heaven is
with your eyes.

I remember it clear as day…
8pm, Wednesday, August 12, 2015.
I was sitting near the view site
overlooking Pacific Coast Highway.
The summer solstice of the night.
You stared at me as if to say,
I love you.
Why are you doing this to yourself?
Josh, why are you killing yourself
one hit, one drink at a time?

I didn't understand the rainbow
floating on the ground, blessing
my shoes.
I thought you were forcing me
to pick up my mind-made feces.
Smoking woe,
I wandered.
Misunderstood

by you, by myself, by God
which I didn't really believe in,
like the rainbow.

I've seen sky give birth to rainbow
a pointillist Pollock
exploding knives into an *ensō*.
But I didn't understand myself,
my actions and your sadness.
As I sat there,
smoking woe.
Not knowing why I was so sad
and why
you seemed to echo my mirage.

Thank you
for giving me that look,
for puncturing my whole universe
with your eyes.

Thank you
for believing in the rainbow,
even when I thought I was a piece of shit
trampling all over myself.

Thank you
for warming me up on nights
when I felt like carrying suicide on my shoulder.

Thank you
for burning a sad look of *I love you*
into my heart,
which still burns.

When I Think of You in Tears
—for Bingo "Batman" Corwin
By: Joshua Corwin

I still remember your face.
They said you were gone.

I didn't believe them.
Sometimes, I still don't.

I could have named you anything.
And you could have been the soul
to provide shelter
for any little boy or girl.

God didn't have to send a sign
and write a lamppost on this highway,
saying heaven is here
on four legs.

And I don't know why I'm writing this letter,
as I stare into the fire—
years later,
as the thunder strikes windowpanes
of the heart.

And I just want to reveal oceans,
arms outstretched
with cupped hands,
my psalmic palms crying.

Yes, my hands are crying in the night.
And although years have passed,

I still think of you
from time to time.

I embraced manhood in your stars,
your irises beckoned me
one last time,
as the injection of serenity painless—
they said it was painless,
but I winced for you and wept in disbelief.
I saw your eyes twitch,
your head tilt.
I know the living don't die.

Notification

On the death of Soledad

By Douglas K Currier

I told the leaves. I told the squirrels.
I told the thunder, the fireworks, the cap
guns that they could no longer startle you
onto the couch or under my chair. I told
your leash. I told your squeaky toys
– the elephant, the turtle. I told that bitch
veterinarian that kept us waiting, even when
we didn't feel well, so many afternoons.
We've paid all of the useless medical bills.
We no longer spend much time in the backyard.
Now, we pull the couch in front of the door,
so that perhaps we'll hear someone who wants
to force his way in. That was your job.
I've told the couch. I've told the rug
in the upstairs hall. I hear you sometimes
at night still. I've told the birds.

Soledad

By Douglas K Currier

In old age, to care for me, comes pure soledad
– a daughter, left behind the others, a sure soledad.

This daughter, the plain one, wants more, wants
a name. "Name me." she says. I say, "You're Soledad."

My age wanders the night streets late and watches lights
in windows. I go out to come home to demure Soledad.

My age sits on park benches, at bus stops, on curbs
and watches young men that might lure Soledad

out of my keeping, night sweats and sounds, the ache
and the thoughts of how long to endure soledad.

This daughter just smiles, shakes her head, continues
alone and knows she'll become a mature soledad.

This old man I am, sits in drawers at the table.
This daughter, a chair, an embrace can cure soledad.

For Halo
By Candice Louisa Daquin

My debt rests in your fur.

As they light it, and it burns, and your form shrinks from this world

your black and white paw, limp against my clutching fingers, wishing you would stay

those images, they are not my friend as you were my friend

I imagine what you feel and then recall, you no longer feel anything, though that does not seem right

without religion I am left unknowing, where you land next or if you will awaken in paradise or remain slumbering

whether asleep or in a void, if we can truly leave, and have nothing of ourselves remain, but ash and debris

it seems impossible that you were once, jumping onto the table and making me laugh with your antics, only to be nowhere and gone eternal

I may not possess sufficient faith, but your energy stays like stillness in this empty house and from the corner of my eye

I still see your shadow slink by, just as my grandmother's voice is pitch perfect in my head. Is that imagination or wishful?

Or do ghosts haunt us willing supplicants? A bouquet of delusion to soothe our empty arms? Or will you live forever within me?

And when I take my turn at the Ferris wheel, our nothingness will reside near one another. I like the idea that all I have loved will, mingle as returned starlight in the ether and touch one another with reminder for being alone or worm food is a cold dinner companion I wish not to believe in.

Your fur was thicker than all the cats here, who grew up hot and listless on porches

you came with me in a pink plastic box, obscene in its garishness we laughed, putting it through customs, the harried lady at flight desk remarked; *well, there he goes,* as you were hand delivered, to the pit of the plane

I worried because I wanted you to be on my knee, but; *no madam, I'm afraid for long haul he must ride in cargo and don't worry few of them get upset*, as if she were crouched among you, knowing this

and this seemed false, as so many things do, when big decisions linger like absent friends, at the periphery of moments, too quick, too big, for staying still.

Briefly I wondered: Should I really be moving? To this strange country I do not yet know and burning bridges indefinitely?

It felt as wrong as right ever was and I stood in the airport watching the thin man take you behind a curtain and then as you were on your way so was I.

You see …

I took my cue from you, quite often and of the two of us, when we landed, I think you looked less bedraggled while I fought with immigration because one of my papers, was not 'just so' and they called and fussed, because immigrants are not very welcome in any country.

When we reunited, on different soil with the sound of cicadas or crickets, you were hot against my grandmothers' blanket and had peed, because they don't let animals out to the bathroom at 30,000 feet

me, younger, naïve, pursuing dreams, while you imagine mice or pigeons and later lizards and snakes, as you learned the ways of the desert

perhaps the tenor of your meow changed, to reflect the inflection of your adopted country. It may seem easier, but it is not easy for any of us who come by boat, plane or smuggled, to lands not our own. We each bring with us, that belly full of ache

and you were always able to soothe mine, with your purr and reminder of our start, beneath colder skies and smaller streets with little houses and narrow rooms

where we knew our place … and here? We could only speculate, or clumsily test our sea legs against the strangeness of being, with mistake and estrangement, our sole friends quite a while.

Unable even to drive, I walked you down the road for your first vet check and people gaped from their large cars at the floundering foreigners walking where no-one walks and everyone uses big trucks to go one mile and purchase a giant Sippy Cup and some Ding Dongs, things with names that sound fun and 40 additives

my kind of humor and banter lost against surge of habit, the vet seemed surprised I had carried you rather than driven and tut-tutted

at your lack of dental hygiene but remarked how beautiful your thick fur was, how cats in these parts tend to have snakeskin, we all laughed at that, even you cast a fisheye his direction, like you possessed the real secret.

I remember those exploits and driving to Canada on another exodus, when stateless, we began again another groove in our fitful recording

the deep snow and your paw prints leading me nearer and further, like ice fish, we swam in our odd circumstance

in cold you slept beside me and purred in your sleep to the sound of icicles warming and falling into snow, the sky a heavy weight holding its breath

eventually we returned to the place of infernal heat and sizzling sidewalks where only us and straggly weeds dared to step.

Years wound like lost yarn beneath our odd foray, until you were old and fragile and I barely noticing, because I did not want to believe you could quit being the little cat, in the pink plastic box, glad to see me at the first airport in our new world.

It was naive or immature of me to forget, cats' lives do not echo ours and mine seemed suddenly far too long and yours, bitterly short

a terrible echo of inequality, I did not have the strength to imagine losing you, when together we always were.

Even people who wrote said; *'Dear Candy, Dear Halo'* as if they could see the join of your fur and my skin against the other

I told myself I would be there when they sent you to that place I could not follow, despite knowing in my mind the terrible pictures, would roam long and unbidden for many years

to look into your eyes and remind you how much you mean to me and always how I will look for you, until we are reunited and then I expect

all this will be mere bad dreams and again we can go forward, or sideways or whatever direction the after world takes us

but please together, is all I want. For with you gone, I wait without watch, an absence greater than anguish, for you were my best friend in this lonely world, assuaging the hard edges and frayed corners

we came here together and still I am more lost without you than when I arrived, for your bright eyes and happy tail gave me courage Halo, and ever shall I look for you coming into the kitchen in the morning with your half howl of greeting starting my day and ending it with putting you to your bed

never once thinking there could be a time when you were not, and I still went on.

Aristotle said it best: "A relationship is two bodies, one soul, that is real love, and we are floundering when absent from one another"

like the ice fish when it warms up, and water is all, but gone.

For Stella
By April Garcia

It's been
4 years—
yet, I remember.

Vet calling.
Said, you couldn't walk. Back legs, stiff
 —falling over.
Nerve damage.

Large tumor
in your neck
pressing

on your spine
 —the likely cause.

More humane
to put you down

than prod

your failing body
like a pincushion.

Do you want to be here?
I didn't—

 I couldn't.
  Coward.

Eleven years
—you were mine.
How could I watch

you take your final breath,
chocolate brown eyes closing—
like warblers
before a storm.

Sapphics For a Crow

By Claudia Gary

Caw! C-caw! you shout from above the chimney,
warning, scolding, flaunting your height, haranguing.
What could be so serious and for so long,
   crow on the chimney?

Cheep! Ch-cheep! he cries by the basement window,
first attempt at using his wings like Mother's
failed. He's angry, hungry and scared, defeated,
   chick by the window.

Caw! you now interrogate me from on high:
Why this stupid house where there once were arbors?
Why that trench, the window-well trap I can't reach?
   Crow on the rooftop,

here I go to offer your chick a tree branch.
Will he climb it? Oh, but he trembles, backs up,
turns around and presses his beak securely
   into a corner.

I withdraw and hope he'll escape in secret.
Out in front, three lavender plants have withered.
Prying up their brittle gray roots, I toss them
   into a corner.

Next day there's no cawing, no wind, no cheeping.
Lost? Survived? I may never know, but someone's
found the lifeless lavender stubs and placed them

back in their garden.

Mother crow, you've left me a gift! But what for?
Caw! C-caw! A mockery? Grieving? Thank-you?
Thanks for what? For trying? Succeeding? Failing?
   Seeing things your way?

You Once Were Many
By Amata Natasha Goldie

You once were many, but now you are few,
Now, you are refugees in your own land,
Your families were lost as you fled,
Your forests burnt to the ground,
As the winds howled,
Carrying the screams of death,
Throughout your once green paradise

You are our furry friends,
Our feathered friends,
Our scaly and winged creatures,
You dwell in the native bushland of Australia,
Keeping the balance of the ecosystem,
Tending to your families,
Fleeing from predators,

But now blackened bush, like sticks of charcoal
Are the remnants of your homeland,
And whole generations of species
Are no longer,
Stolen by the tsunami of the fires that spread relentlessly
And those that remain have become refugees
In their own land that once supported life

Once there was a symphony of cicadas and birdsong,
And a gentle rustling through the bush,
As the furry friends made their way through,
Now there are no animal homes,

No nests for the birds,
No branches for the koalas,
No greenery for the kangaroos,
No food, and no peaceful place to rest upon

The elders know this land,
A sacred connection, unbroken
But this ancient knowledge, is not consulted by the laws of the West
And 46 million acres were burnt,
And one billion animals were lost,
And fires burned not for days, or weeks, but months
And we as a nation, mourned your loss

You are our winged, scaly, furry and feathered friends
You once were many, but now you are few

Paws Healing The Earth

The Feline Teacher
By Amata Natasha Goldie

How many lifetimes have I lived
To reach this feeling?
How many times have I looked
Through different eyes,
With the same soul?

And each time,
The eyes have seen further and opened wider,
Until the distant horizon is reached,
In only a blink,
And voyages of lifetimes enter the realm of yesterday,

I see infinity in your eyes,
And a mystery that defies all understanding,
You are the embodiment of a world beyond worlds,
Yet you dance in the eternal moment,
With your playful innocence,

You teach me the art of being,
And of playing,
Of living in the ever-new moment,

To tiptoe in twilight,
And frolic in the morning light,

How many lifetimes have you lived, Beloved?
To teach me this, in your unconditional ways?
How many times have you lovingly taught

The same lessons,
So that we may all be free?

And each time, it is your own eyes,
That have truly seen,
And it is your own heart,
That has opened wider,

Until the suffering and sorrow of humanity,
Is no more,
And in those eternal moments of your love,
The whole planet is healed

~ Dedicated to my Beloved feline teacher 'Tibet'

Floppy-Eared Free Loader

By Albert Gonzalez

Mom finally said yes!

For two brothers—
one big,
Mikey sick

Puppy dog
protector

Bought him from
some chump off the road

Scrap joined our family

Barked all night
fulfilled little boy's dreams

Precious nights
can't get back

Get up!
Look after this floppy-eared
son of a bitch

Tore everything up
backyard bound
Jumbo head
scared everyone on the block

He got so big
you got so sick—

I remember you
gazing out the window
beaming at Scrap

he jumped at you—
ready to play

Scrap and Mike
never saw each other again

Never understand—

Mom and I
kept Scrap fed

We took turns staying
at home—

at the hospital—

Scrap barked for Mom

Floppy-eared
freeloader
and me
Smoking on the patio
drunk as shit

Days go by

Mikey died—

Outside
wanted to cry with my Scrap

Never saw him again

He was gone

Paws Healing The Earth

Satchel

By Marian Haddad

When you would stand outside the glass door, door framed in wood, you, having been out in sun, some minutes, not near an hour.

I would have thought you'd prefer to stay outside a little longer than that, but when I'd pass by, I'd see you, standing, facing the glass, waiting for me to see, waiting for me to know, you were ready to step in.

Satchel, you elegant, old soul. There you were, almost human. Patient. Standing in place, as if ready to wait until you had to. As if you'd just come home from work, dapper, you knew your homeplace. You preferred the cool inside of it all. Sprawled there, on the leather couch, almost not large enough——for you.

I remember the night, when I had no house to go to, your mother allowed me in. One night, it was just you——and me, and Timmy D. We watched him play; by then---you loved me much. Your warm body leaning in---to me. I leaned back in——to you. Silken, I could feel your ribs as I'd rub the side of you; how you loved your human.

Bonnie

By Marian Haddad

More than one thing, in common.

Us.

Once, you were young as your owner, hair as platinum.

Once. I saw her, your human mother, at a distance, I heard the familiar name, ring.
Holcombe. And her, a stallion. Tall. Proud. Brilliantly beautiful.

You absorbed her.

What we become. What we keep.

Keeping your space sacred. Okay with alone. You did not need banter.

Like her, your body——slowed. Went quiet. You stuck to yourself——your master, her son.

You, waiting for his arrival, at the front window, looking---
You invoked him. Wishing him——there. Oracle. The power of purpose.

Once, when I was the only human, near you——you came to me, without announcing. Quiet, in your surety.

You sought me.

Me, reclining, double doors, half-open. You came, across tiled floor, I heard you trying---to stand, trying to make it——all the way——to me. And there, you settled. At the entry. My breath, surprised, replete. Your desire, to come. Maybe you knew——you were leaving.

Smokey in the Year of Our Feline, 2099

By Lois P. Jones

The cat carries sycamore leaves on its wet back to the edge of rain, then curls on the teal velvet chair into a roundness she wants to rest inside. The half circle of spine, moon flecked and soft as sin. All day the water batters eaves and satins the windows. All day and often an eye opens like a sleepy lizard small at first and then wider, a bolt to the cosmos because cats are not from here. Their eyes a window to a future metropolis where people move along steel streets in black catsuits, silent and surefooted. Candles grow along the country roads and oh the lakes, the lakes are silvered with the fins of fresh tuna. No sallow skies or oil slicked fields. No disease hunkered in square inch hours waiting to pounce.

The Goodmorninggoat Says
By Lois P. Jones

what are you doing inside the house all alone?
The goodmorninggoat sings
Joan Baez's *Hello in there, Hello.*
When it rotates its eyes like a strange planet,
when it bows its head, it sees ten times more than you.
When he grazes he keeps an eye on the world
so you don't have to.
The goodmorninggoat wants you to come out
and play at being goat for a day,
kick up your back legs (or your sad little two)
and chomp on the dry grass outside your door.
The goodmorninggoat says eat an entire rose
and your soul will rain in petals
your hooves take root in belonging.
The goodmorninggoat goes with you
as you take a step back onto the land.
He likes the wind in the trees.
Butts your hand for goat pets.
The goodmorninggoat asks:
who will scratch the place between my horns, please!
I need you.

All Our Little Ones?
By Zilka Joseph

they think I'm some kind
of evil being winged and vicious
how is that possible?
Look at me look at me
I'm tiny and furry and brown
and have small mouse ears
eat insects that no one wants
and all I ask is a place to hang
upside down and sleep
I'm just a flying mouse really
I make babies like they do—these
creatures who build huge
houses and cut down
all the trees take away our shelter
but even if we fly
far far away from them
and their bald backyards
to find some wooded niche
or some cracked rock or hidden
cave to live
they come to smoke us out
raining hammer blows
on us as we fall
like ripe plums

laughing cheering
they smash our skulls
wipe us out
in one fell swoop murder yes murder

families no whole colonies
do you know even their cats
can drag us out of hollows
with their long curved claws
and eat us alive
yes the button-sized new born
cling to still warm bodies
of their dead mothers
as they are devoured
no one but us who are half dead
hanging on by our nails
can hear the high-pitched cries
of all our little ones
day-old shiny pin-sized eyes barely
opened and shut
one moment a heart beat-beating
the next a smear of blood
they have stolen our breathing
can you hear the two-legged beasts
inhaling
our children's breath

Black Swan

--Australian exhibit, Kolkata Zoological Gardens

By Zilka Joseph

Oh regal captive

is this your man-made fate

swimming in your stale pond
sailing close to the concrete edge
of its kidney-shaped loops
diving in with your scarlet beak
flashing like a flag
your sleek shape tilting over
to feed on vegetation
suspended limply
in the murky pool

Is it just me who thinks

this is wrong maybe
you are quite at peace here
being fed and on show
for noisy crowds
and gawking school kids
Are they as dazzled by you
as I am when I see you rising
from slimy water

a goddess clad in midnight

feathers glistening
like a black sun
Algae shimmers in green
sequins over your closed
wings so when you preen
you are a queen stroking order
over your body
your beak smoothing

every quill and feather Oh you beauty

you who once came from a spark of life
an egg a chick a wild creature

meant to be free do you even know
what freedom means
are your siblings in this prison too
were you hatched here
in Kolkata or magnificent bird
were you stolen as a fledging
snatched as an egg
from your home
far far away Down Under

In Taos Pueblo, Suddenly
By Zilka Joseph

stones ring, the ground
shudders with the sound of some heavy,
hoofed animals thundering
towards us. Two shadows

appear across the stream splitting
the pueblo fields in half. We
see their enormous
heads clearly now. Two horses
with eyes wide and inky
staring like the windows
of the mud dwellings
that rise in silhouette
behind us. As startled

as we are
they are poised to
run away from us,
alien beings invading
their land. One horse is
grey, dusty mottled,
one appaloosa-ish red,
both unbridled, rider-less,
winter coats thick clumped,
burred; manes heavy,
matted here and there, flow
over the bridge of their necks.
Late morning light
marbling their backs, they

stand fifteen hands at the shoulder,
look down at us like gods. Mist
rises from their coarse hides.
Then lulled by silence, or perhaps

our stillness as we hold our breath
among the red willow
shoots and skeletons
of cottonwoods
at water's edge,
the dark beams of their eyes

reach into us
like lasers, search us,
but find no tricks, no guile,
no Trojan betrayals.
Eyes soften, and I can
almost hear their hearts
slowing down, as ours do.

Then, they drop their mighty heads
to the silver-braided water,
and drink for a long
time. Heads
bowed, we wait.

Ten Haiku from Madagascar

By Abhay K.

a red fody
sitting on a bare tree
singing

fighting each other
for mating
mouse lemurs

secreting honey dew
in the baobab forest
white flatid bugs

giant eggs in drawing rooms
where have all
the elephant birds* gone?

morning to evening
poetry of hoopoes
what do they sing?

wandering at night
in Masoala rain forests
aye-aye*

roaming the sacred spiny forests
in south Madagascar
radiated tortoises

calling out
to walk barefoot
the tsingys* of Bemaraha

a haunting hum
fills the Andasibe*
Indri Indri*

twin ring-tailed baby lemurs
clinging to their mother's fur
a hungry fossa lurking around

Elephant birds* were giant flightless birds that once lived in Madagascar but are extinct now

Aye-aye* is a long-fingered species of lemur active at night

Tsingys* are forests of limestone needles

Andasibe* rainforests are located in the east coast of Madagascar

Indri Indri* is the largest species of surviving lemur. It is critically endangered.

Midsummer Night Walk
By Diane Kendig

At sunset we note
the Coventry Crazy Man
circling and recircling the block,
a June 22nd so hot,
it's dog days a month early.

Our two dogs run and duck
while we, dog-tired, play watch-dogs,
smile, forget ourselves;
we've gone to the dogs,
and they'll let us lie.

"Why 'Emma' for your new dog's name?"
he asks. "It means 'healer'," I say.
"Like on a leash?"
"Like in a wound."
"Maybe she'll do both."

The sun bleeds to its place
on this longest day.
From now on, shorter, darker.
And the real heat.
I follow Emma home.

Paws Healing The Earth

The Geese at the Prison

for Lu Capra

By Diane Kendig

We look for them like weather or mail,
so close to the road we see
each regal neck and goose squabbles for corn.
All October their inky bodies blotted the green,
and the inmates said, being fed,
they would roost here all winter.

Four months they've huddled
in the blond-stubbled white field.
A few rangers made V-flights
to Blue Lick Road and back
as we've returned each week,
and last week, returning, witnessed, I swear,

a thousand rush up and circle the lot,
applaud the air and stop the light with wing clutter.
In the dimness they called out
their beauty and wildness
the unnatural naturalness of their ground,
and they rose, not out, but above it all.

"The Geese at the Prison" by Diane Kendig from Prison Terms. (Main Street Rag, 2017).

Her Name Was Candy

By John C. Mannone

She was a breech birth
    but this blue baby
        whale managed to slip
into ocean

and take her first breath
    through the blowhole, fresh
        as peppermint. Her skin,
smooth as caramel

not scaled with barnacles
    like her mother's
        or scarred with whale
killing teeth of Orca.

Being underwater
    wasn't too different from
        the ocean in her mother's belly
with slow waves

of uterine heartbeats.
    She remembers.
        She's a survivor.

Soon she would sweep
    krill through her baleens,
        visit the kelp forests
that shadow a darkness,

a darkness she'd know
    nothing about—
        the irony of mankind
and his appetite for extinction.

Now she sings
    her own haunting whalesongs,
        her own cries for help
echo in an empty ocean.

*Author's Note: "360,000 blue whales were killed in the 20th Century in the Antarctic alone. The blue whale has a truly global distribution, occurring in all oceans except the Arctic, and enclosed seas. But despite this, they are one of the rarest of the whales, numbering between 10,000-25,000." (World Wildlife Fund)

Raccoons Can't Fly

By John C. Mannone

The cottonwood I lived in as a child was a comfort
when I found out I couldn't fly. I couldn't fly away
like those yellow-bellied sapsuckers did. I never saw
a prairie sky so overcast with yellow-green before.

Momma hurried, nape of my neck in her gentle mouth,
hid me in a hollow trunk, heartwood of that Kansas tree
rotted out. The maddening shuffle of a locomotive
wind howling in its tracks, churned the ground. Its wrath

blew tons of dust against the cottonwood—breaking
above where momma covered me deep into that old
tree hole so the suck of wind wouldn't sweep me
into blackness. It swallowed her instead. Aching,

I think about her whenever I see a cottonwood standing
in a breeze, its serrated leaves quaking, breathing.

Kiko in Greenville

By Ellyn Maybe

a million saw you fall into the world
sleeping 5 minutes dreaming the symphonic horizon
earth cam made you an incredibly adorable superstar

kiko in greenville
you have a twitter account
born in autumn to a giraffe named autumn
you have a facebook page

5 feet 8 at the moment of birth
what makes your heart quiver?

squiggly ear curious taller than a kaleidoscope
what sort of thing inspires you?

do you ever wish you were a person?
people! do you ever wish you were a giraffe?

kiko of greenville, you are sooo lovely
eating the leaves from the trees of the giants
seeing the love in everybody's eyes

calm presence in a clackety clack world
a living origami painted by van gogh

kiko, someday i'll see you and we'll dream of
xylophones and music way up high in the sky
and the world goes on and on

Two Samoyeds

For Lisa, Hannah, and Abby

By Christopher Merrill

Here's little Latte,
Queen of Java,
Eating pâté,
Eating lava.

She's white and round
With eyes like coal;
Her tail is wound
Up in a scroll.

She bites our ears
And chews our toes—
A pair of shears
On pantyhose.

She barks and jumps,
Piddles and poops,
And then she humps
The nightstand—whoops!

And when she sleeps
She dreams of cats,
And chimney sweeps,
And cricket bats.

But once awake
She licks our faces—
O for God's sake!
Off to the races.

~~~~~

Queen Cappuccino is no more.
Her days of sprawling on the floor,
And chasing cats to the ravine,
And howling at a TV screen,
Came to an end on New Year's Eve.
What a good dog. It's time to leave.

The nights of sleeping on her back,
Paws twitching in her dreams of black
Cats trapped in a mulberry bush
And the quiet child who liked to brush
Her thick white coat smoother than silk,
Have gone the way of all our ilk.

What remains? Tufts of fur; her collar,
Tags, and leash; one pig's ear. This dolor,
Which may define the year to come
In grief and memory: the sum
Of what we saw once here below—
A puppy playing in the snow.

The Takins At Thimpu

By Jagari Mukherjee

(At Motithang Takin Preserve, Thimpu, 1995)

I held out my palm full of chestnuts.
I was shy. So were the golden takins
as none approached me,
until the young, brave one, half my size,
saw me and sauntered over.

His eyes were liquid brown with trust.
He put his soft, warm mouth against my palm
and ate the chestnuts slowly,
like a well-mannered guest.

I dared not move,
for I feared to disturb the moment
quiet like the Himalayan snow in winter.
That afternoon a precocious teenager
learned, the meaning of tenderness.

*The Takin, a rare mammal, is the national animal of Bhutan.

In Krakow Zoo

By Kunwar Narain

Translated from the original Hindi by Apurva Narain

Even though he lives
In a grand zoo abroad

He is utterly alone these days
Ever since his consort expired

He moves in circles for days on end
Like a madman in his patch

One is curious to know all
That goes on inside him…

From his wet eyes he looks
Like a poet,
From his probing trunk a scientist,
From his forehead a thinker,
From his ears a sage:

If this were it, he would have been
The scribe of the Mahabharata

> But immersed in a sadness
> Even an elephant
> Looks so human

* *In Indian mythology, Vyāsa dictated the Mahābhārata to scribe Ganesha, the Hindu God with an elephant head*

*From the book '*Kunwar Narain: No Other World: SelectePoems: Translated by Apurva Narain*, 2008, Rupa Publications, India, and 2010, Arc Publications, UK.'

Bears in Autumn

By William O'Daly

Whose eyes cool among the flames?
What is this hunger, the calm roiling the pond,
refusing to burn with the thicket
like the names of those forgotten?

They are excited, the young bears, heads emerging,
swimming with the white and blue currents of beginning—
they leave the forest, the cave of white light, no longer
underground.
Mama trudges because she must—protecting, helpless.
We stare at them, see what they want us to see—
could the Big Dipper be anything but a dipper?
But to the Romans it was Bear or Seven Plowing Oxen,
and now, to the Europeans, Ursa of the Hour is a plow.

They say a trinity of bears still rules
over the earth. But can we be certain
it has only one body—could it be ours?
We burn with the same conviction,
our faces open as we pick up the axe
and go about our father's business.

Originally published in an earlier version in Tiferet Journal: Fostering Peacethrough Literature and Art, Fall 2016, print and online.

Heron Dances Over the World
By William O'Daly

Even you're not watching
as you spread your black tattered wings
and step among the colors of the physical world—
spindly legs conjure the symbol for infinity
in red earth, in fresh blue snow and white mist.

Endangered islands bloom, the wetland fills
with mountain shadow. In a parallel universe
your reflection moves to its inner calling,
to folded granite, music of the waterfall.

You live as hidden origami, with creases
and abandon, intricate patterns that resist
the receding shore. You circle like an equation
neither eyes nor lips can touch—motion that can't be solved
or written on the tongue. You do not stop to preen
among the battered dunes.

Your cry wrings iron from irony,
recalls the silent bells, laments the love
I've forgotten. You breathe closer to the swaying aspen
than to the orphaned moon and the tide's pull.

In this dance you create like a beetle
your own being.

*Originally published in Life and Legends, Inaugural Issue, Summer 2014; then in Sacramento Voices, Cold River Press (anthology), 2014

Did you ask the tree?

By Yogesh Patel

A blackbird had lost interest in a song.
For it knew it wouldn't be ever heard.
A tree is nothing but a cacophony.
There, more birds than leaves you'll find.

A blackbird knew her story wouldn't be told!
Lone singer, it will never be heard.
To perch on a tree and sing was once a bond
with you. Now the Ustad-Sagird Tombs.

A blackbird drops dead, unknown.
There are no tombs; that's the jungle-culture!
The earth takes back what it gives.
You call out names: villain or martyr.

There were more birds than leaves on a tree.
No one asked the tree if it were happy...

Blueprint

By Saleem Peeradina

He wears the brick wall-paper of skin wound
Around his body like a crossword puzzle.

Taking baby steps to stand upright
Finds him crumbling to the ground
Like a pack of cards. Reshuffling
Hooves, spine, belly, neck, he rises
Like a pyramid on stilts. Ready or not,

This architecture of mismatched limbs – one of
Evolution's surrealist pranks – has equipped
Him with all the grace of a creature
Designed to race across earth's stage
For ever vertical. Giraffes are known
To graze, sleep, mate, even give birth standing up.

Since that is what they do best,
He is even better off standing still, posing
For a Dali painting:

A pair of horn-stubs mushroom from his head,
Ears cocked, for signs of danger. Yet, he's not shy
Eating out of your hand, furry tongue scraping your palm,
Jaws moving gently like a cradle rocking. Nose sniffing
The air, eyelids drooping; uncertain of being at ease
In this wilderness, the steeple of his neck arches skyward.

Donkey

By Saleem Peeradina

Take an animal – a strong, smart, intelligent creature
who has endured human bondage for thousands of years –
turn him into a beast of burden, then use his name
to mock or malign people. So he's not handsome
like a horse but is funny-looking with floppy ears
and a head too large for his body. So his braying may not be
as melodious as the calls and cries of his captive cousins.
He is meek and docile and easily tamed. But that's his
undoing. He does not protest, no matter how large a load
is heaped on his willing back. He puts up with verbal slurs
and under duress, nods along to the sting of the whip.
It would seem he *likes* human company. He is calm and gentle
with babies and children. He's been called stubborn
but that comes out of an instinctive sense of preservation:
he will not venture where the path is unsafe or the road
dangerous. He is nothing if not dependable. He can be trained
to protect other livestock. He is a reliable carrier of produce
to the market and he can transport even heavier loads
like wood, water, bricks, and quarry stones. He knows his
mission. So head down, he plods along, in step with
the one he regards as his brother.

Door

By Robert Pinsky

The cat cries for me from the other side.
It is beyond her to work this device
That I open and cross and close
With such ease when I mean to work.

Its four panels form a cross— the rood,
Gatepost of redemption.
The rod, a dividing pike or pale
Mounted and hinged to swing between

One way or place and another, meow.
Between the January vulva of birth
And the January of death's door
There are so many to negotiate,

Closed or flung open or ajar, valves
Of attention. O kitty, If the doors
Of perception were cleansed
All things would appear as they are,

Infinite. Come in, darling, drowse
Comfortably near my feet, I will click
The barrier closed again behind you, O
Sister will, fellow mortal, here we are.

"Door"— first published in The New Yorker on April 2, 2001, it appeared in my 2007 book Gulf Music as part of the sequence "First Things to Hand."

Advice to the Dog Sitter

By Connie Post

Remember the house key
is never where you left it

remember the pull of the leash
and how it reminds you
of the long sinew of muscle

remember how to zip your coat
with one hand

remember he is a stray
that he has only been with us
for thirty six days

remember sometimes
he does not believe
the truth in the cracks of night
or that we will wake
in the morning
and offer sustenance

remember how your whole self
can be found in the fur
at the underside of his neck

remember that language
is the illusion of intimacy
how a tepid silence
has a buoyancy of its own

remember there is mercy
in your broken hands
and he will pull from you
whatever you have to offer

*Originally published in the Comstock Review &
Also published in my first full length book, Floodwater*

The Night Before Surgery
By Connie Post

Take the dog
on a long walk

the one where you pass
the old metal bridge
beyond the area
marked with "mud slide " signs

watch his footsteps carefully
and he will help you
find the places
to hide
when you
enter that long
languid
journey of anesthesia

watch the way
his fur mingles
with the slight breeze
how he follows the faint edges
of a gravel path

feel the cadence
the rise and fall of his lungs
and tell him
you will see him there
on the ledge of solitude
and remember
he will teach you
everything about the anaphora
that stays in the body
that stays beneath your skin
only as apparent
as faded scar tissue
or mercy

Originally published in the Kentucky Review/ and in my second full Length collection Prime Meridian

"Terriers Hold Grudges" Our veterinarian says

By Connie Post

When we get home
you hide under the table
punishing me
with your obsidian eyes
and ears flopped over your face

I go to you
find the place you are hiding

I tell you
"I know they treated you bad before
but this is us now"
and tuck my fingers under your chin

I think about the long scar
across your ribs
when I adopted you
I think about the paperwork , stating
"over 100 taken
from a dog Hoarder in Bakersfield"

I think about how you
protected us
against two boxers
who attacked us
last summer
I wait for you at my desk
while I busy with paperwork

and slowly
you huddle at my feet
find small ways
to forgive me

I break open a new bag of dog snacks
while old grudges crumble
and your leash
is quietly put away

I Have No Horse
(for Teddy)

By Jennifer Reeser

Return with racing hooves. I have no horse,
for long ago, I gave away the stable
you bought for me. I had become unable
to work them to a lather on the course.

Recall with fond approval, how each fall
and winter, through till spring, the Navajo
and I were so responsible, to go
and empty every steed and pony's stall,

to ride and ride, around those steep and slick
layers in the land, where Man had dug
to strip it of its riches, with a shrug --
in order that his sons had salt to lick.

Come back with two strong stallions we can ride --
O brother of my mother, Lonesome Bear --
or I would be as happy with a mare,
as long as she keeps steady, and in stride.

The Mockingbird
(Traditional Acoma Pueblo song, translated)

By Jennifer Reeser

Morning comes and mockingbird speaks and sings.

Mornings, mockingbird is singing, speaking

Songs for the benefit of human beings.

Mockingbird, Mockingbird, regularly singing

Songs for the benefit of humankind.

"No, not the monkey, Mother, but the stag..."
By Jennifer Reeser

"No, not the monkey, Mother, but the stag,"

she says to me, and pierces through my ear

the steel post of a golden-antlered deer

which mirrors that upon my shoulder bag.

"That is your spirit." Fabric patterns zag

in zebra prints around us. Leopard spots appear --

the creatures of Rwanda and Zaire.

Behind her words, the seconds seem to lag.

Here is a novel view with which to cope:

for her, I am fragility and grace --

the esoteric watcher in the wood,

the neutral mover. *Bambi Antelope,*

I tell myself, "Pull your poker face.

Your fawn has followed you and understood."

Billy

By Susan Rogers

"Your cat is a person in a fur suit," my former neighbor Jamie told me. His name is Billy, but she called him William. I never knew where he went at night until I discovered he was sleeping with her. They watched TV together and she told me he had a favorite show: "Sex in the City." "He likes to watch himself in the mirror," she said. When she moved out he waited at her door for months. He likes beautiful women. He loved my last roommate and would sleep entwined in her arms. Last week as I walked to my car, another neighbor whom I do not know stopped me and asked, "Are you with Billy?" I wondered how this girl knew his name as he does not wear a collar. She said, she had heard I did some healing work and asked if she could come by. I found out that Billy has been calling to her from the bushes below her second story window. She comes when he calls to her and she calls down to him. Then they have a conversation. Like Romeo and Juliet. Her name is Sapphire. She texts me to ask about Billy. And I send her pictures of Billy. I try not be jealous. He is a cat, after all. One day I will ask him his secret.

summer serenade
my cat sings to my neighbor
I do not wait up

"*Billy*" was previously published in *Eclipse Moon: 2017 Southern California Haiku Study Group Anthology*

Blessing at Fair Oaks

for Tina

By Susan Rogers

You smile into the oaks and even a dark, ghost-filled ravine turns fair. I walk the climb with you passing that place where old trailers and broken furniture, piles of abandoned books share space with a rock strewn road. Looking over a sun- kissed hill, last of the day's light lingering, dusk blanketing the green below, I see warmth still glowing in your fine, blond hair. In your eyes, the late afternoon, clearest blue. I gaze with you and your Katrina rescue dog. High on the hill, we chant an Amatsu Prayer above the chaos and smog of an ordinary, city day. I snap a photo of the two of you. But I cannot tell who has rescued whom—the dog and you, this place and I, all rescued, each by each. With love we breach the dark, reach out in light, offering to the earth, the sky.

twilight hush
winging into lavender
two birds in tandem

Previously published in What the Wind Can't Touch: 2016 Southern California Haiku Study Group Anthology

Rough Win

By MistyRose™

Good grief Charlie, the cat lady said it,
Lucy continued, as if she's the head medic,
How now can you be brown and insane,
Mad canine teeth froth at mouth, not brain.

Wolves wouldn't heel and had no fetching name.
Then they lost the wild call that sheds no blame.
Now they are snooping around the promised land,
Out of the doghouse, sniffing behind, and front of hand.

Tail thumping joy at an opened door betrays a nose in the air.
No solitary cat ruling the bench would ever judge that fair.
And another crying kitten would not need to be set free
If it had heeded the warning barking up the wrong tree.

Who needs to be on a hot tin roof over a cozy rug?
No loose strings must attach to claim it a free hug.
Domestication rumbles, until an alternative seeks to please.
Naturally, on such an occasion someone cuts the cheese.

Guarding a fox from a henhouse would now seem strange.
Deer, antelope and tom cats remain at home on the range.
When can openers go down, no tranquil cat will claim its pride.
But all in the family, a dog, looks after its litter while inside.

Felines prefer limp liquid lines on charcoal art wafers
To scratched wad sculptures of laid down papers.
People of some breeding might make the switch.
Puppy love greetings even kiss Lucy the bitch.

Turf Wag-ing

By MistyRose™

I'm at the end of my rope in a dark corridor.
So that is where I fall in the pecking order,
A-stray, the top of their food chain.
When can I exit the doghouse for dam and dame?

The priorities of all but the kitchen sink
Get their pass through fence and chain link.
The tail was wagging the dog.
Who's dog is it: Asleep like a log!

This mutt won't enter another's fight.
Light prevails ceding battles out of sight.
Final terms leash lasting rights
By closing off those nights.

A Peacock's Feather
By Minal Sarosh

When a tree is a tower
and a tower is a tree,
does the peacock know
there are no branches?

When it trapezes on the metal bars,
when it calls out to its mate
does the peacock swoon,
 dizzy with the heights?

When the thunder clouds
come, and rain lashes down
does the peacock fear for its nest
dangling without shade?

Yes, maybe by now
entangled in cables
the peacock already knows it
that a tree is a tower
and a tower is a tree.

And when I pick up
its rainbow feather
fallen in my balcony
I know it too.

Honey
By Minal Sarosh

As suddenly as my muse appears
out of nowhere the hive appears
sticking to the ceiling of my mind,
an overturned hanging mound of wax.
From where did it come overnight?
Did it come to bring me luck?
I keep wondering as through the days
the bees keep hovering like words
around me, then like tiny flying saucers
smoothly land in the open windows
in the honeycomb of my thoughts
buzzing, feverishly working
like obsessed clones, fanning their wings
adding sweet sentence after sentence
picked up from the garden of flowers,
till my poem begins to flow
like liquid amber, sweet nectar,
and when I dip my finger in the honey,
lick a drop of the golden sunshine,
I taste the sky, I taste the rainbow,
I taste life itself.

Animal Fare

By Kedarnath Singh
Translated from the original Hindi by Kalpna Singh-Chitnis

One November evening,
truckloads of bulls are going for sale
in Dadari fare.

The bulls coming from Punjab are
tall and muscular.
They will sell at the price of horses.

It's fascinating to see how
the bulls can outshine the Mustangs.

The trucks, covered in dust,
are running at a fast pace.
They need to arrive at the fare in time.

The bulls standing for hours are weary and tired.
They stare blankly.

A jolt tinkers the bells they wear
in their necks and startles them.

They look at one another
as if asking, hey brother,
how far is the fare?

Five Puppies

By Kedarnath Singh
Translated from the original Hindi by Kalpna Singh-Chitnis

She has given birth to five healthy puppies,
beautiful, soft, squishy, and fluffy.

They stand in confusion
taken by surprise,
cooing in light,
as if asking the sun -

Here we are, tell us now,
what to do with the world?

Paws Healing The Earth
By Kalpana Singh-Chitnis

It all comes back like a cascade flowing
no one forgets the way back home.

The beauty of the wild isn't the flowers and trees alone
more, it is the scent of the forest.

Walking from the trails to the cliffs,
from the den to the river

I find my footprints everywhere,
on the rocks, in the mud, and dusty trails.

My handprints stamped on the trees
wave me from a distance.

The vision blurs, but the time does not fade anything.
How many times I have climbed to the top and fallen to perish

only to rise again. The memories surface,
like white clouds form in the turquoise blue sky.

The moon rises on the pale dune, and my spirit howls.
Welcome back! The animals weep in joy.

'O eternal me! I have returned home.
My feet are paws healing the earth.

Epiphany
for Troy

By Kalpana Singh-Chitnis

If I were to trust my intuition,
you were the hunter cougar
I fed my flesh to as a novice monk.

In nighttime, we went on the same track,
one looking for food, and the other for water
in a perennial forest, our home
on the edge of Siam and Myanmar.

It had been a century. I had almost forgotten, but you
remembered to return, printing your paws
on the trail, we had left behind,

following the imprints subtle in our minds to redeem.
Your eyes burning with compassion, like lanterns
lit in the darkest of night, kept me warm, until the day
you melted away in the flux of our tears.

In a deep-sea that no one can fathom but you and me
I see you lying on the bed like a luminous pearl
in blue light, sleeping in the shell of my memories.

Naming

By Kalpana Singh-Chitnis

The day you arrived,
it was the night before Christmas.
You were a gift from Santa for being good to your kind.

You had come to me nameless
loveless, mother had abandoned you
and those who owned her
had abandoned you twice.

How could a mother be so callous?
She didn't look for her pups.
Was she sadder than you were?

How could you possibly know,
you were too young to understand.
Shivering in the winter rain, hungry and alone
you were found under a truck.

At least, this is what I was told.
Your siblings weren't found. They were taken.
You were the runt of the litter. No one wanted you.

Precious diamond, you were meant for me.
The destiny had dragged you to me by its chain,
collarless, hurting in the pain of neglect, right when
my hands were ready to cradle another life.

Cooing in agony, you sat in my lap
nipped my finger while feeding you bread.
But I wasn't upset. I knew you were sad

hungry for love, thirsty for the milk
dripping from your mother's breast.
But your tongue, so young and tiny,
was unable to latch from afar.

You licked my hands profusely.
Your anxiety was nothing but a desire
heightening with the pain of separation.

But she wasn't supposed to come back.
You had to learn how to live with your pain.
Same as *He did, waiting in heat and frost,
rain and storms, year after year

watching the trains come and go,
at a station, for someone never to arrive.
I could see His reflections in your eyes

living a pain over again, melting in sorrow,
silently in my hands, like Him in earth's lap,
on a stormy night, covered in snow.
He extinguished like a candle, lit in you now.

I pull a warm blanket for you in a hurry.
I spilt in pain, thinking of him
and kiss you.

Paws Healing The Earth

I shed the tears you couldn't,
I erased the years, no one should
ever wait for anyone,
and named you – *Hachi*.

*He is referred to as the legendary Japanese Akita dog Hachikō, also known as Hachi, remembered for his exceptional love and loyalty to his owner, for whom he waited long years following his death.

Red Fox Family

By Kalpana Singh-Chitnis

Do you hear the sound of snow falling?
The wind whispers into her fuzzy ears.

She opens her eyes a little and closes.
The furballs tucked under her belly suck the nectar of life
keeping one another warm, in a narrow den.

Do you hear the sound of her babies' breath?
I ask the winter and snowflakes.

Encounter in Whitehorse

By Adrian Slonaker

Under cloudlike clouds too thick
for the aurora borealis to penetrate, the
Yukon River crackled a greeting beneath its
icy shell while log-cabin skyscrapers and
silvery evergreens slept or possibly
played possum.
The coyote, whose furry
ears rose at the terminus of a frosty road,
filled the night with its answer:
nip-nip-nip.
Not a baleful howl or a gritty
growl, just the
nip-nip-nip of playfulness and pep,
the tiny grin in its voice mirrored
by the one on my face.

The Wolf On My Right Arm

By Adrian Slonaker

The wolf on my right arm-
the dominant one-
appeared upstairs in a Newfoundland
tattoo parlor while I spied seagulls gliding
above the chilly coastline.
The wolf meanders in the moonlight in search
of sustenance just as I
seek meaning in midnight musings.
The wolf pursues pack play or
gambols alone just as I
hobnob with buddies or savor
restorative stretches of solitude.
The wolf is filleted as a threat to those who
don't fathom its ways just as I've been
slapped with the suspicions of
the closed-minded.
The wolf on my right arm displays
gray-blue eyes wet with sweat just like
the ones irrigated by my tears.

Doggerel for Lily
By Donna Snyder

I

The dog's bumps grow.
I say one is because she's extra sweet.
One because she's pretty. Another
because she's so clever

The cave-in above her eye
I cannot disguise as a gift of any kind.
I kiss her sweetly. Tell her the lie I told
another honey child,
You're gonna live forever, baby.
You're gonna live forever

II

There once was a hero Mother award to the proletarian who bore
the most children to be proud soldiers in the ongoing Revolution.

I told Lily she's the hero mommy.
Her breasts hang down like soft velvet.
She even has two extra brown nipples
on her spotted belly.

All her babies stolen and sold.
Her left to starve.
Her set for execution.

Her with her lumps.

I sob into her fur,
Thank you, baby, for coming to live with me.
You're the hero mommy.
When I cry you rub my cheek with your face.

One day you will be gone.
One day my cheek will be bone.

Lover boy

By Donna Snyder

My dog Sparky was a lover boy. He
followed me from room to room, always at my feet
or reaching to hide his face in my chest. We called him
Mr. Velvet, because he was soft as night and twice as black.
When he was six months old a new neighbor had a pup,
a Rottweiler. Jada was a few months older,
black, beautiful, and big with a booming puppy voice.
Sparky, who tried to ignore my boxer sisters, was besotted.

Sparky taught me what "love sick" means. He
and Jada would lie on either side of the fence touching noses.
For an hour or more they would lick and kiss through the wire,
like teenagers sticking their pink tongues in each other's mouth.
He would whimper and whine when Jada had to go inside.
When I would call him to bed, he would lie there and groan,
great big deep sorrowful moans, his wails vibrating his chest.
He would flop onto his bed in disgust and cry for love.

Sparky taught me what "puppy love" means. He
was smitten. One day Jada escaped her yard,
running for the park when we caught her. We
brought her into the yard to wait for the neighbor.
The puppies ran and played. She nipped his ear,
made him squeal. He didn't mind. He took Jada
into his doggie condo, showed her his private pool
in the tin tub under the mesquite, the one his alone.
He let Jada sit in it and play splash.
He ran to fetch but let her give it to me,
their muzzles touching on either end of the stick.

Sparky loved Jada so much he even let her near me.
He let her lick me and bowl me off my cinder block perch.

Sparky taught me what "broken hearted" means, too.
The neighbors moved. Jada was gone. Sparky grieved for days.
Too morose to play splash.
Too despondent to play fetch.
At night he would cling to my legs and mournfully low.
The sound began in the chest, an almost indiscernible growl,
crescendoed into a howl, finished with his nose beneath my thigh.
Then he would give a lovesick sigh and settle into dreams of Jada.
I knew because he whimpered in his sleep.

Blue Eye of the Magpie
By Megha Sood

Hope lives in the blue eye of that magpie
twittering each August
the beliefs dissolve:
riding on the molten sun rays

rubbed by the laughter of the gentle wind
hidden in the thick canopy of the trees
Of that mighty oak standing for eons
hiding the pain in his thick branches
/where all pain has been knotted in its deep trunk/

giving sustenance to the tangling vines
embracing the strong arms of the oak
a reflection of hope:
a birdsong is broken into million pieces
a lost serenade

the empty nest with the broken egg says it all
and the oak stands mighty tall
a mute spectator

Pain is hidden in the
blue eye of the magpie
carried by the broken leaves of the fall.

Animals Within Us

By Janaka Stagnaro

Upon this world shaped with love so round
A great host of animals can be found
Eagles majestically soar through endless skies
Lions roar with courage in their eyes.
And cows slowly graze luscious green fields.
All live in us as we act, think and feel.

The Cow
By Janaka Stagnaro

Upon hot plains
   or near mountains of snow,
Mother cow you chew
   round and round and slow,
As perfect as the course
   the planets row,
From your patience
   your milk ever flows.

Frey the Cat on a Solstice Night

By Janaka Stagnaro

In the cold and darkest night,
To curl beside the firelight:
To purr, to twitch, to dream my dreams.
Ahh! a bowl of chocolate mice-cream.

Give me a lap or a soft rug will do.
A Saucer of milk--all I need from you.
My life is simple; I hope you see.
Love is truth, as three is three.

You humans, I do not know,
When darkness comes, the wise go slow.
Yet you scurry from store to store
To celebrate this time with gifts galore.

Now, little humans, do try and see;
But being not cats, you might disagree.
Drop all names or this day you'll lose:
Christian, Pagan, Atheist, or Jew.

So many words, yet nothing you tell.
To catch your bird--be quiet and still.
Hear the songs of this magical night.
The rekindling of hearts, the rebirth of Light.

Tour of Grief

By Melissa Studdard

All seventeen days the orca wore
her dead like a crown,

sorrow riling to a bob and weave,
knocking her hollow.

What water and womb
could no longer carry, she had to carry.

We watched through binoculars
as if distance

were real. As if we
were not also tottering

on the head of an exhausted,
grieving mother. As if we were not also

becoming too cumbersome,
too heavy to bear.

*Previously published in Kenyon Review

Because Deathbolts Illuminate the Wonderstorm

By Melissa Studdard

Cruel, the highway that
took the dogs.

I've seen its shoulders
convulse gently in the crying of nightfall

the way a teenaged girl can be
both vicious and vulnerable.

It doesn't like what it has done,
and I don't like to say it.

Sometimes I hold a kaleidoscope
to my beloved's eye
and ask him
to never look at anything again
but me.

How can I trust a world
that hasn't yet
honored the softness in his pupil?

Is it possible to protect those we love?
To protect anyone?

I plant plum trees in his heart.
I devour his fruits to the pit.

Love is sometimes a stay
against insanity.

The dogs, it was my fault.
Trying to help, I scared them
into the rush.

I live it over and over.
The way a body can spill
like sunlight
from its skin.

Previously published in The Missouri Review

There's a brightness folded into every bird

By Melissa Studdard

but the bird doesn't know it. The bird is thirty
birds who soared out of dreaming to invent
sky, thirty birds flying in the formation

of a bird. God tells them, Open, O moon-beak
O silver-black O sliver of luck, and the bird says,
Break me until I'm whole. God says, Empty,

and the bird spills a splendor of jewels from
their thirty beaks into the valley. Don't think
I'm a diamond, God says, Find me, and hands

the bird a map back to the inside of its own
bone, then disappears. But the bird doesn't
understand the quest(ion). Thirty birds split

into a thousand that search under everything—
stone, fabric, sun-face, gold—until they find
no god. Now the beak yells, Take me; I have

no reason, and an arch of wing lifts sun-up
towards light, and a thump under the chest
answers, Yes and yes and yes and yes.

Previously published in chapbook Like a Bird with a Thousand Wings (Saint Julian Press) and The Nervous Breakdown

Gaze of Horse – Lure of Wholeness
By Ambika Talwar

Gaze into horse eyes. Wind laughs! Pulls our hair.
Presses feet into earth burnt by Sun's ancient tales.

Something stirs – shall we dream it into surrender?
Shall we rise to zenith in beauty with infinite joy?

Horse will turn away if we are untrue to essence.
 Bruised, let visions arrive… Let flow old sorrows

into earth, re-seed muted call of distant drums.
Inner fire renews hymns. Listen to the scales.

Listen to horse heart – rhythms of hooves in unison
as mountain wind wildly curves tales around us.

Lore of horse thrills in us light-flooded halls;
Ache sharpens fingers as we revise our being.

Wild equine poised for flight reveals grandly
despite wooly fear, we can tenderly hold hands.

We can re-discover places famished under caverns
 of our heart, where thorns or stones grow forgotten.

Horse, cosmos, gardens, flutes, love, forests, trees
greenly full of pine, poems, words, drumming...

Stories of wounds melt as horses push away grime.
Let us recall pristine cantos of wild men and women.

These are paths to love, to illumination, to loyalty, partnership, fulfilment, beauty, peace ... freedom.

Gaze into horse eyes. Wind laughs! Pulls our hair. Silence stops everything. Taste lure of freedom.

Mystic companion of our wholiness, horse inevitably commands attention: Gaze with horse at trillion stars.

Where you used to
for Kobuk

By Leslie Thomas

Each pocket holds a stale treat, a leash remains
in my car back seat, gold shimmers in wool

where you used to be. Anxious prints are still
on the sliding glass door.

Walks are numbered now; first, second, third
on the Kinnickinnic trail alone, hands untethered,

my gait feels lumbered, I learned these paths
through you. A narrow depression calls,

I wade through dead leaves and dense grey
stalks of last year's sedges.

You loved the spring mud, I follow deer scat
to a fast-moving stream, sit on a fallen silver maple.

Branches span from bank to main current, I think
we belong to riparian margin, swirling ephemeral gurgle.

You are like this old bark, altering flow after life.
Soon, purple-stemmed aster and marsh marigold
will burst from loam, secret trails will smother
in prairie cord grass and big bluestem.

At our bench overlooking the broad river valley
it is quiet, I imagine you seated near, scanning

the horizon, the air for scent. Ears perk
as trumpeter swans honk, Canadian geese yip

in altitude. Whistling yellow warblers sing
boundless and clear, I try to catch your pitch.

The Persistence of Torture

--The satyr Marsyas was skinned alive after losing a musical contest with Apollo. Punished for his ambition, Marsyas, in some versions of the story, was the true winner.

By Lee Upton

The dog violet, pressing a flat ear to the ground,
has news of great importance:
it is spring
and jealousy turns its blade again.
First a prick at the neck and another nick and then
Marsyas's eyelids are peeled
so he can't help but see as
they flay the fur off him
and pull down the map of his body
and curry his skin into
a canal. Steam hisses off the oiled husks of him.
What do the executioners expect to find,
unwrapping their prize?
His executioners take their time slitting his groin,
calling him a woman and laughing,
as if they own forever what he can never be again.
His blood rains into the storm-blue eye of the violet.
They work at his thighs until the flesh
slides to his ankles like a stocking.
His hooves dance in the sloughed off rind.
There are jokes. I'm sure of it.
Even as the onrush from what's loosened gives,
as if a musician must be
poured from a kettle, but first
scalped, grated,

scraped into paste,
oh he's bled—he's dressed like a doe in a shed—
and saddles of his own skin surround him.

Thus, the satyr became human,
as did his torturers,
as did music.

Every spring the dog violet shrinks closer to the earth,
 once again washed in the memory of the thundercloud
of Marsyas's body,
and so the violet turns humble,
spreading its kind across the grounds to escape
the punishment for making beauty that
humiliates a power
that won't be humbled.
Skinless, to be human,
to break membranes,
fear wiping its hands over your eyes,
and now so many silences:
those we can't hear
and those we try not to hear
and those beneath
what's heard.
In some myths,
a reed or laurel or blossom
fills to the brim with a soul.
In this story silence pours into silence,
and silence turns into music made of silence—

What will hold the dog violets back this year?
A scout has broken from the ranks.
The leaves flicker with Marsyas.

Paws Healing The Earth

He was an animal, like us.

The extinct, those that no longer
bend down the grasses
or the tree tops or
curl in a wave
or draw their roots into the soil—
Marsyas and his kind are extinct.
Apollo is extinct.
Beside the limestone quarries the cry violets
lifted their lavender-colored faces:
the cry violets are extinct.
The earthly music of the extinct,
those wild beings skimmed off the earth,
scoured—
the blade so thin
and the scald—
in the encyclopedia of the extinct,
and in human music, that silence.
The satyr's skin drying, tacked to a pine:
the tattery flag of the extinct.
He was not our savior, not a traitor either.
We can only try to imagine Marsyas's music,
his gift.
We are his skin now,
his animals, his herd.

That music,
the wound in the dog violet,
the stillness there,
as if whatever living thing that lives in silence
witnesses how living skin
is thrashed

wild with misery.
It is always happening:
the persistence of torture,
the extinguished music,
the ones made strange to us
skimmed off the earth.
The grass turns gray,
the decayed trees creak like wicker.
Executioners
stand back
to admire their work.
Wasps crawl
across a tender body, a body
made infinitely more tender
in sunlight,
the heart still beating.
Some traditions hate us.

What do we call
those who went ahead,
our scouts, the extinct?
They didn't ask to be named.
Now we know them only as words.
Marsyas, revolutionary, belongs to us and the other animals.
The animals of ourselves listen for his flaying,
even now the blade pressing up against
every shape his mouth makes.
A thousand traps cannot snare the spring,

or close his raining eyes,
or stop the wind through the pines where he's howling.

Previously published in The Boston Review online—

THE TITLE POEM

Paws Healing The Earth

By Kalpana Singh-Chitnis

It all comes back like a cascade flowing
no one forgets the way back home.

The beauty of the wild isn't just the flowers and trees
it is the scent of the forest.

Walking from the trails to the cliffs,
from the den to the river

I find my footprints everywhere
on the rocks, in the mud, and dusty trails.

My handprints stamped on the trees
wave me from a distance.

The vision blurs, but the time does not fade anything.
How many times I have climbed to the top and fallen to perish.

The memories form like white cloud fragments
in the turquoise blue sky.

The moon rises on a pale dune, and my spirit howls!
Welcome back! The animals weep in joy.

O eternal me, I have returned home.
My feet are paws healing the earth.

"Animals are such agreeable friends—they ask no questions; they pass no criticisms."
-George Eliot

Contributors' Bio Notes

Jonel Abellanosa is a nature lover and an environmental activist. He loves all animals, particularly dogs. He loves to self-study the sciences. His poetry collections include *"Multiverse"* (Clare Songbirds Publishing House, New York), *"Pan's Saxophone"* (Weasel Press, Texas), and *"50 Acrostic poems"* (Cyberwit, India).

Shanta Acharya is the author of twelve books, her latest poetry collections are *What Survives Is The Singing* (Indigo Dreams Publishing, UK; 2020) and *Imagine: New and Selected Poems* (HarperCollins Publishers, India; 2017). www.shantaacharya.com

Leticia Austria, a Native Texan and former opera coach, rediscovered her lifelong love of writing poetry during her subsequent residence in a Catholic monastery. Her work has since been published in print and online publications. She has received awards from *The Lyric* and Utmost Christian Poets. She now resides in Olympia, Washington.

Mark Blickley is a New York widely published author of fiction, non-fiction, drama and poetry and recipient of a MacArthur Foundation Scholarship Award for Drama. He is a proud member of the Dramatists Guild and PEN American Center and author of *Sacred Misfits* (Red Hen Press), *Weathered Reports: Trump Surrogate Quotes from the Underground* (Moira Books). In his 2018 video, *Widow's Peek: The Kiss of Death,* was selected to the International Experimental Film Festival in Bilbao, Spain, was an Audie Award Finalist for his contribution to the original audio book, *Nonetheless We Persisted*, and co-curated the Urban Dialogues art exhibition, *Tributaries: Encontro de Rios*, in Lisbon, Portugal.

Betty Burton is a country girl from Virginia who became interested in storytelling by listening to her Daddy regale the family with his stories. Stories became her passion. She was thrilled when she learned to read and write. It was a new delight to see her stories/poems come to fruition. A stroke interrupted her writing because she was a lefty but never giving up she taught herself to use her right hand. She loves her cats and kittens and extends her love for all animals.

Jenna Butler is the award-winning author of six books of poetry and essays, including, most recently, *Revery: A Year of Bees* (Wolsak & Wynn, 2020). She is a professor of creative and environmental writing at Red Deer College in Canada, and runs an off-grid organic farm.

Jennifer Carr is an EMT, firefighter, author, and poet living in Santa Fe. When she is not working, she spends her time reading and writing poetry. Her work has been published in print and in online publications.

Xánath Caraza writes for *La Bloga, Seattle Escribe, SLC, and Monolito*. For the 2018 International Latino Book Awards, she received First Place for *Lágrima roja* and *Sin preámbulos/Without Preamble* for "Best Book of Poetry in Spanish" and "Best Book Bilingual Poetry." *Syllables of Wind* received the 2015 International Book Award for Poetry.

Joshua Corwin, a Los Angeles native, is a neurodiverse, Pushcart Prize-nominated poet. His book *Becoming Vulnerable* (2020) details his experience with autism, addiction, sobriety and spirituality. A UCLA lecturer, published alongside Lawrence Ferlinghetti, Corwin hosts the "Assiduous Dust" podcast, writes the Incentovise column for *Oddball Magazine* and teaches poetry to neurodiverse individuals and autistic addicts in recovery at The Miracle Project, an autism nonprofit. Corwin is the editor and producer of *Assiduous Dust: Home of the OTSCP*, Vol. 1 (April 5, 2021) featuring 36 award-winning poets, demonstrating a new type of found poem he invented. www.joshuacorwin.com.

Douglas K Currier has published work in many magazines both in the United States and in South America. He lives with his wife in Carlisle, Pennsylvania.

Candice Louisa Daquin is Senior Editor at Indie Blu(e) Publishing and a Psychotherapist. Indie Blu(e)'s anthology SMITTEN won finalist in the National Indie Excellence Awards and The Kali Project, a collection of Indian women's poetry has just published worldwide. Daquin's poetry is available in most bookstores and she is a long-time animal rights advocate and vegetarian.

April Garcia is born and raised in South Central Texas. Garcia's work has appeared in multiple anthologies published by the Laurel Crown Foundation of San Antonio, Texas and Southern New Hampshire University. Her work has appeared in Northwest Vista College's *The Lantana Review*, and online with SNHU's *The Penmen Review*, and *Unlost Journal*.

Claudia Gary teaches villanelle, sonnet, and meter "crash courses" through writer.org and elsewhere. Author of *Humor Me* (David Robert Books, 2006), chapbooks including *Genetic Revisionism* (2019), and poems in journals and anthologies internationally, she also writes chamber music and science articles. See pw.org/content/claudia_gary; follow @claudiagary.

Amata Natasha Goldie is an Australian poet and author. Her compositions are woven around the central themes of love, unity, consciousness, and our eternal nature. She has written unpublished collections of spiritual poetry, prose, and soul affirmations. You can find more of her offerings here: https://ashramoftheethers.wordpress.com

Albert D. Gonzalez is an author and poet. He writes poetry about the realities of life, loss and struggle. His poetry challenges what grief means when you lose a younger brother and the financial setbacks you face on a daily basis through the eyes of a Mexican-American.

Marian Haddad, MFA, is a Pushcart-nominated Syrian-American poet, writer, and manuscript & publishing consultant. She earned her B.A. in creative writing from The University of Texas at El Paso and her MFA from San Diego State. Her work has appeared internationally from The Middle East to Brussels, Belgium, and in assorted anthologies via small presses including Milkweed Editions and a number of university presses. Journals in which her work has appeared include Crab Orchard, Kenyon Review online, Mizna, and Bat City Review. She is the author of the poetry collections, Saturn Falling Down, Somewhere between Mexico and a River Called Home (a Small Press Notable Book), and Wildflower. Stone. (endorsed by Pulitzer poet, Yusef Komunyakaa). She lives in San Antonio, where she is working on 12 books of poetry and essays. Her manuscript clients and writing students have won varied awards and fellowships. She has been writing since the age of six, where she first began transliterating.

Lois P. Jones's work featured in a 2019 film adaptation by the Visible Poetry Project. Awards include the Lascaux Prize, Bristol Prize judged by Liz Berry and Terrain Prize (finalist) judged by Jane Hirshfield. She hosts KPFK's Poets Café and is poetry editor for Kyoto Journal. *Night Ladder* was published in 2017 by Glass Lyre Press.

Zilka Joseph, educator and manuscript coach, has been published in *Poetry*, *Kenyon Review Online*, and *Poetry Daily*. Her chapbooks *Lands I Live In* and *What Dread* were nominated for a PEN America and Pushcart award, respectively. Her book *Sharp Blue Search of Flame* (WSUP) was a Foreword INDIES prize finalist. www.zilkajoseph.com

Abhay K. is the author of nine poetry collections, most recently of *The Alphabets of Latin America*, and the editor of *The Bloomsbury Book of Great Indian Love Poems, CAPITALS, The Bloomsbury Anthology of Great Indian Poems* and *New Brazilian Poems*. He has translated Kalidasa's *Meghaduta* and *Ritusamhara* from Sanskrit. His poems have been published in several literary journals including *Poetry Salzburg Review* and *Asian Literary Review*. His 'Earth Anthem' has been translated into over 50 languages. He has received SAARC Literary Award 2013 and was invited to record his poems at the Library of Congress, Washington DC in 2018. His forthcoming collection of poems is titled *The Magic of Madagascar*.

Diane Kendig's five poetry collections include *Prison Terms*, and she co-edited the anthology *In the Company of Russell Atkins*. She has published poetry and prose in journals such as *J Journal, Under the Sun*, and *Ekphrasis*. She curates "Read + Write: 30 Days of Poetry," now with over 4000 subscribers.

Sandra Kingery is a Professor of Spanish at Lycoming College, Williamsport, PA. Kingery has published translations of two books by Ana María Moix, as well as a translation of René Vázquez Díaz and Daniel Innerarity; and a number of books for Xánath Caraza, HUDSON, among others.

John C. Mannone has recent poems in *North Dakota Quarterly*, *Foreign Literary Review*, and *Le Menteur*. He was awarded a Jean Ritchie Fellowship(2017) in Appalachian literature. He edits poetry for *Abyss & Apex* and other journals. A retired university physics professor, John lives near Chattanooga, Tennessee www.jcmannone.wordpress.com www.facebook.com/jcmannone

Ellyn Maybe has performed her poetry all over the country, including Bumbershoot,the Poetry Project, the New School, Taos Poetry Circus, South by Southwest, Lollapalooza, Albuquerque Poetry Festival and Seattle Poetry Festival. She has also read in Europe at the Bristol Poetry Festival, on the BBC, and in poetry slams and readings in Munich, Frankfurt, Hamburg and Stuttgart. She opened the MTV Spoken Wurd Tour in Los Angeles. In addition, she has also read at USC, UCLA, CSUN and Cal State Fullerton, among other colleges. Writer's Digest named her one of ten poets to watch in the new millennium. Her work has been included in many anthologies, including Word Warriors: 35 Women Leaders in the Spoken Word Revolution, Poetry Slam, Another City: Writing From Los Angeles, Poetry Nation, The Outlaw Bible of American Poetry and American Poetry: The Next Generation. She was on the 1998 and 1999 Venice Beach Slam teams. She was seen reading her work in Michael Radford's (Il Postino) film Dancing at the Blue Iguana.

Christopher Merrill has published six collections of poetry, including *Watch Fire*, for which he received the Lavan Younger Poets Award from the Academy of American Poets; many edited volumes and translations; and six books of nonfiction, among them, *Only the Nails Remain: Scenes from the Balkan Wars, Things of the Hidden God: Journey to the Holy Mountain, The Tree of the Doves: Ceremony, Expedition, War*, and *Self-Portrait with Dogwood*. His writings have been translated into nearly forty languages; his journalism appears widely; his honors include a Chevalier des Arts et des Lettres from the French government, numerous translation awards, and fellowships from the John Simon Guggenheim Memorial and Ingram Merrill Foundations. As director of the International Writing Program at the University of Iowa since 2000, Merrill has conducted cultural diplomacy missions to more than fifty countries. He served on the U.S. National Commission for UNESCO from 2011-2018, and in April 2012 President Barack Obama appointed him to the National Council on the Humanities.

Jagari Mukherjee won the 2019 Reuel International Prize For Poetry, and the Tagore Literary Prize 2018 for Book Review. Her chapbook Between Pages was published by Cherry-House Press, Illinois, USA, in June 2019. Her latest book published is The Elegant Nobody by Hawakal Publishers in January 2020.

Kunwar Narain (1927–2017), an iconic figure in Indian literature, is considered one of the finest poets and thinkers of modern times. His diverse oeuvre of seven decades, since his first book in 1956, includes three epic poems, eight poetry collections, translations of poets such as Borges, Cavafy, Herbert and Różewicz, and books of stories, criticism, essays, diaries, and writings on world cinema and the arts. His accolades include the Sahitya Akademi award and Senior Fellowship of India's Academy of Letters; medal of Warsaw University; Italy's Premio Feronia for world author; the civilian honor Padma Bhushan; and India's highest literary prize across all languages, the Jnanpith. A reclusive writer, some of his works remain unpublished.

Apurva Narain is Kunwar Narain's son and translator. His books include a translated poetry collection *No Other World*, a co-translated story collection *The Play of Dolls*, and a forthcoming book of poetry translations *Witnesses of Remembrance*. His work has appeared in numerous journals such as *Asymptote, Modern Poetry in Translation, Poetry International, Asia Literary Review, Indian Literature, Scroll, Two Lines, Columbia Journal*, etc. Educated in India and the University of Cambridge, he writes in English and has professional interests in the fields of public health, ethics and ecology.

William O'Daly has translated nine books of the poetry of Chilean Nobel laureate Pablo Neruda, the most recent a finalist for the 2018 Northern California Book Award in Translation. O'Daly's chapbooks of poems include *The Road to Isla Negra, Water Ways* (a collaboration with JS Graustein), and *Yarrow and Smoke*.

Yogesh Patel, honoured with Member Of The Most Excellent Order Of The British Empire (MBE) for Literature, in the Queen's New Year Honours list 2020, is a writer, poet and editor of *Skylark*. He runs *Skylark Publications UK* as well as a non-profit *Word Masala* project to promote SA diaspora literature. A founder of the literary charity, *Gujarati Literary Academy*, he has been honoured with the *Freedom of the City of London*. With LP records, films, radio, children's book, fiction and non-fiction books, and three poetry collections to his credit, in 2017, he was presented to The Queen at Buckingham Palace. A recipient of many awards, including an honour in April 2019 at the New York University as a Poet-of-Honor, he has read in the House of Lords and at the National Poetry Library. His recent collection of poems is *Swimming with Whales*. His writing has appeared in PN Review, The London Magazine, Shearsman, IOTA, Envoi, Understanding, Orbis, on BBC TV and Radio, and more. He is also anthologised in MacMillan, Redbeck and other anthologies. By profession, Yogesh is a qualified optometrist and an accountant. Websites: patelyogesh.co.uk and skylarkpublications.co.uk

Saleem Peeradina has published six books of poetry including *Heart's Beast: New and Selected Poems* (Copper Coin, 2017). He has a memoir called Th*e Ocean in my Yard* (Penguin books, 2005), and has a book of essays forthcoming this year called, *An Arc in Time: Cultural Chronicles from the Last Half Century.*

Robert Pinsky is a poet, essayist, translator, teacher, and three-term Poet Laureate of the United States. Throughout his career, Pinsky has been dedicated to identifying and invigorating poetry's place in the world.

Connie Post served as the first Poet Laureate of Livermore, California. Her work has appeared in *Calyx, River Styx, Slipstream, Spoon River Poetry Review, Valparaiso Poetry Review* and *Verse Daily*. Her Awards include the Liakoura Award, the Caesura Award, and the Crab Creek Review Poetry Award. Her first full length Book, "Floodwater" won the Lyrebird Award. Her second full length collection (also by Glass Lyre Press), "Prime Meridian" was released in January 2020 and was a finalist in the Best Book Awards and the American Fiction Awards.

Jennifer Reeser is the author of seven books. Her most recent collection, *"Strong Feather,"* is forthcoming from Able Muse Press, 2021. *www.jenniferreeser.com*

Susan Rogers, practitioner of Sukyo Mahikari considers poetry a vehicle for light and a tool for the exchange of positive energy. Her poetry is included in numerous anthologies and journals including, *Altadena Poetry Review, California Quarterly, Kyoto Journal, Saint Julian's Press, San Diego Poetry Annual: The Best Poems of San Diego, Tiferet.* Watch "The Origin is One" at https://www.youtube.com/watch?v=rzPA9zeC0Qc She was interviewed on KPFK by Lois P. Jones and nominated for a Pushcart in 2013 and 2017. Listen to her poetry at https://www.loispjones.com/susan-rogers/

MistyRose™ poetry is published in 4 hard-cover anthology books at the United States Library of Congress and in academic journals. She is the only accepted "Spoken Word Artist" in the state of Oklahoma on the Poets & Writers Directory http://www.pw.org/content/mistyrose_ok . She was the Featured Guest Poet in Houston in 2014.

Minal Sarosh is an awarded Indian English poet and novelist. She won the Commendation Prize in the All India Poetry Competition 2005 of The Poetry Society (India) Delhi. 'Mitosis and Other Poems' is her first poetry collection and 'Soil for My Roots' is her first novel.

Kedarnath Singh was a Hindi poet, critic, and essayist. He received India's highest literary honor, the Jananpith Award, and the Sahitya Academy Award. His anthologies include *Srishti Par Pahra, Abhi Bilkul Abhi, Zameen Pak Rahi Hai, Yahan se Dekho, Akaal Mein Saaras, Baagh,Tolstoy aur Cycle, and Matdaan Kendra Pe Jhapki.*

Kalpna Singh-Chitnis is an Indian American poet, writer, and Editor-in-Chief of *Life and Legends*. Her works have appeared in notable journals like *World Literature Today, California Quarterly, Indian Literature, Pirene's Fountain,* etc. She has authored four full-length books, and her poems have been translated into many languages. Her poetry collection *Bare Soul* was awarded the 2017 Naji Naaman Literary Prize for creativity. Her poems and translations have been included in several anthologies. A former lecturer of Political Science, Kalpna Singh-Chitnis holds a degree in Film Directing from the New York Film Academy and works as an independent filmmaker in Hollywood. Her forthcoming full-length poetry collection *Trespassing My Ancestral Lands* is in the making. Website: www.kalpnasinghchitnis.com

Adrian Slonaker crisscrossing North America as a language professional, Pushcart Prize and Best of the Net nominee is fond of owls, opals and *The Alfred Hitchcock Hour.* Adrian's work has been published in *WINK: Writers in the Know, Ariel Chart, The Pangolin Review* and others.

Donna Snyder founded the Tumblewords Project in 1995 and still organizes its free events in El Paso, Texas. She has three poetry collections. Donna's poetry and prose appear in journals and anthologies. She adopts both from the shelter and from the streets, with a particular affection for elderly and ailing dogs.

Megha Sood is an Assistant Poetry Editor for the Literary Journal MookyChick and a Literary Partner with the *"Life in Quarantine"* Stanford University, USA. Her works are widely published in literary journals and anthologies, including Better than Starbucks, Gothamist, Poetry Society of New York, Madras Courier, Borderless Journal, WNYC Studios, Kissing Dynamite, American Writers Review, FIVE:2: ONE, Quail Bell, Dime show review, etc. Three-time State-level Winner NAMI Dara Axelrod NJ Poetry Contest 2018/2019/2020 and First Place National Winner Spring Robinson Lit Prize 2020, Finalist in Pangolin Poetry Prize 2019, Adelaide Literary Award 2019 and Erbacce Prize 2020, Nominated for the iWomanGlobalAwards 2020, and many more. Works selected numerous times by Jersey City Writers group and Department of Cultural Affairs for the Arts House Festival. Editor of (*"The Medusa Project*, Mookychick) and (*"The Kali Project,"* Indie Blu(e) Press). Chosen twice as the panelist for the Jersey City Theater Center Online Series *"Voices Around the World."* She blogs at https://meghasworldsite.wordpress.com/ and tweets at @meghasood16.

Janaka Stagnaro is the author of *The Teachings of Yama: A Conversation with Death*. And eight other books. He is a Waldorf teacher, artist, storyteller, writer, poet, and spiritual counselor. www.Mindfulness-meditation-techniques.com.

Melissa Studddard is the author of the poetry collection *I Ate the Cosmos for Breakfast* and the chapbook *Like a Bird with a Thousand Wings*. Her work has been featured by *PBS, NPR, The New York Times, The Guardian,* and more. Her awards include the Lucille Medwick Award from the Poetry Society of America, The Penn Review Poetry Prize, and the Tom Howard Prize for Winning Writers. www.melissastuddard.com.

Ambika Talwar is an India-born poet-artist-educator and wellness consultant whose poetry is a "bridge to other worlds." She authored *4 Stars & 25 Roses* (poems for her father) and *My Greece: Mirrors & Metamorphoses*, a poetic-spiritual travelogue. Published in various journals, she earned Commendable Mention in *On Fire Movement Great India Poetry Contest* and an award for a short film. Ambika Talwar also serves on the board of CSPS - California State Poetry Society. She lives in Los Angeles & New Delhi. creativeinfinities.com & goldenmatrixvisions.com

Leslie Thomas coordinates 'Write to the River' dedicated to the Mississippi River. Her article *Writing the River* featured in University of Minnesota's, *Open Rivers: Rethinking Water, Place & Community*. Recent poetry publications include *Planet in Peril* from Fly on the Wall press, and forthcoming in *The Trumpeter, Journal of Ecosophy*.

Lee Upton is the author of fourteen books, including short story collections and volumes of poetry, literary criticism, and essays. Her most recent books are *Bottle the Bottles the Bottles the Bottles: Poems* and *Visitation: Stories*.

~~~~

Troy Singh-Chitnis (April 20th 2006 - November 7th 2018) was adopted from the Orange County Animal Shelter in Orange, California, where he had come as an orphan dog at the age of two. *Paws Healing the Earth* anthology is dedicated to Troy's memories. To learn more about Troy, read the editor's note of *Paws Healing The Earth*.

FORTHCOMING

From River Paw Press

www.riverpawpress.com

Paws Healing The Earth

**Kalpna Singh-Chitnis** is an Indian American poet, writer, and Editor-in-Chief of Life and Legends. She is the author of four poetry books, and her works have appeared in notable journals like *World Literature Today, California Quarterly, Indian Literature, Pirene's Fountain,* etc. Her full-length poetry collection *Bare Soul* was awarded the 2017 "Naji Naaman Literary Prize for creativity." Her awards and honors include the "Bihar Rajbhasha Award," given by the government of Bihar, India, Bihar Shri, and the "Rajiv Gandhi Global Excellence Award." Kalpna's poetry has received praise from eminent writers, scholars, and critics such as Nobel Prize in Literature nominee Dr. Wazir Agha, Vaptsarov Award, and Ordre des Arts et des Lettres recipient Amrita Pritam, Academy Award winning poet, lyricist, and filmmaker Gulzar, and others. Her poems have been translated into Spanish, French, Italian, German, Albanian, Chez, Arabic, Nepali, Hindi, and other Indian languages. Her works have been included in several anthologies. The most recent among them are *100 Great Indian Poems* (Bloomsbury, India), *Unseen* (Skylark Publications, UK), *Collateral Damage, Carrying the Branch Poets in Search of Peace* (Glass Lyre Press, USA), and *Paws Healing the Earth* (River Paw Press). A former lecturer of Political Science, Kalpna Singh-Chitnis holds a degree in Film Directing from the New York Film Academy and works as an independent filmmaker in Hollywood. Website: www.kalpnasinghchitnis.com

www.ingramcontent.com/pod-product-compliance
Lightning Source LLC
Chambersburg PA
CBHW020909080526
44589CB00011B/516